# The CIA

Philip Abraham

Children's Press®
A Division of Scholastic Inc.
New York / Toronto / London / Auckland / Sydney
Mexico City / New Delhi / Hong Kong
Danbury, Connecticut

Book Design: Erica Clendening and Michelle Innes
Contributing Editors: Nel Yomtov and Scott Waldman

Photo Credits: Cover © George B. Diebold/Corbis; p. 4 © ER Productions/Corbis; pp. 7, 13, 18, 22, 24, 28, 41 © Roger Ressmeyer/Corbis; pp. 8, 31, 38 © Bettmann/Corbis; pp. 10, 34 © Jeffrey L. Rotman/Corbis; p. 14 © Bill Varie/Corbis; pp. 21, 36 © Reuters NewMedia Inc./Corbis; p. 32 © Corbis

Library of Congress Cataloging-in-Publication Data

Abraham, Philip, 1970-
The CIA / Philip Abraham.
p. cm. — (Top secret)
Includes index.
Summary: Discusses how the CIA was created and how it functions, as well as what it takes to work for the CIA.
ISBN 0-516-24316-0 (lib. bdg.) — ISBN 0-516-24379-9 (pbk.)
1. United States. Central Intelligence Agency—Juvenile literature.
[1. United States. Central Intelligence Agency. 2. Intelligence service.
3. Spies.] I. Title: Central Intelligence Agency. II. Title. III. Top secret (New York, N.Y.)

JK468.I6 A627 2003
327.1273—dc21

2002010656


Printed in the Mexico.
6 7 8 9 10 R 12 11 10 09 08 07 06 05

# Contents

Y834 MW

# Introduction

When most people think of spies, or secret agents, they think of exciting Hollywood movie characters such as James Bond. These daring characters often get involved in exotic international adventures. They use wacky, futuristic gadgets to prevent power-mad villains from taking over the world. Movie spies often disobey the orders of their superiors. Their actions often attract attention to themselves.

Hollywood spy characters may look exciting on the big screen. However, to the real secret agents of the Central Intelligence Agency (CIA), they are the stuff of pure fantasy. Real spies work hard to go unnoticed. They spend many tough hours studying the details of their assignments. Rarely is the workday of a CIA agent filled with wild car chases,

While Hollywood secret agents such as James Bond are exciting to watch on the big screen, they are nothing like real CIA agents.

exploding bombs, or visits to lush, romantic locales around the world.

The CIA helps the president of the United States and other government officials make decisions about the national security of the United States. It does this by gathering and giving accurate and timely information concerning foreign threats to the United States and its allies. When ordered by the president, the CIA may engage in covert action. Covert action is any secret effort to influence or effect events in another country.

Though most people have heard about the CIA, many do not know exactly what it does or how it works. This is because the CIA must operate in almost complete secrecy in order to protect its employees and allies. Often, when national security is at stake, the last thing the CIA wants is a lot of attention in the media.

This book will take you inside the mysterious and dangerous world of the CIA. You will learn how the

The CIA follows news from all around the world to learn of any potential threats to the security of the United States.

CIA was created and how it works. You will also learn what it takes to work for the CIA. Prepare yourself: you are about to enter the world of real-life secret agents.

Chapter One

# The Information Seekers

The beginnings of the CIA go back to World War II and a man named Colonel William "Wild Bill" Donovan. Donovan had been a colonel in World War I. President Franklin D. Roosevelt asked him to come up with a plan to set up a national intelligence organization. Colonel Donovan developed the Office of Strategic Services (OSS). In June 1943, he was put in charge of the OSS. It was the job of the OSS to give the president and other U.S. policymakers the important facts and intelligence needed to fight and win World War II.

When the war was over, the OSS was shut down. The U.S. State Department took over many of its functions. However, Colonel Donovan convinced President Harry S. Truman that an organization such as the OSS was vital to national security—even

In 1946, Colonel William Donovan received a Distinguished Service Medal from President Harry S. Truman.

in peacetime. In 1946, President Truman set up the Central Intelligence Group. The Central Intelligence Group was replaced by the Central Intelligence Agency on September 18, 1947.

The main job of the CIA is to collect and analyze information about foreign governments. This information includes data about the political, economic, and military operations of other governments. Information that the CIA gathers is called intelligence. The CIA also investigates non-governmental

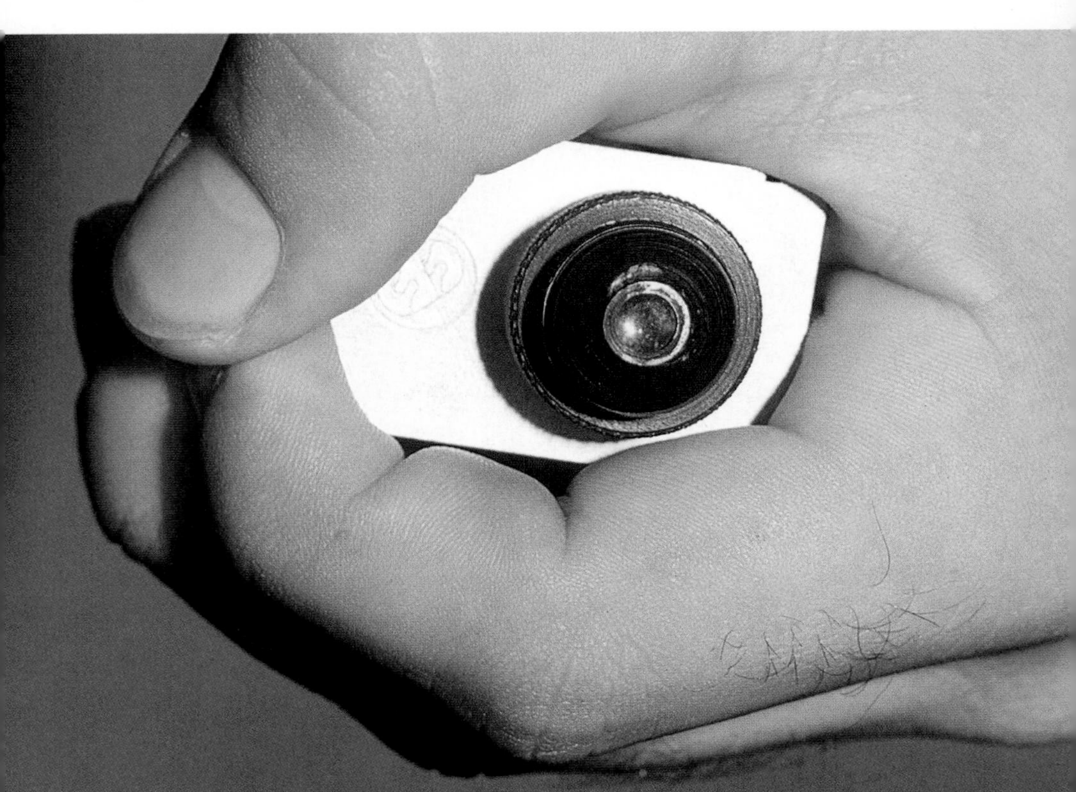

groups, such as ones that take part in terrorism or organized crime. The CIA acts on the intelligence it gathers when ordered by the president or another high-ranking government official. CIA workers refer to this as being tasked.

## MAIN TYPES OF INTELLIGENCE GATHERED BY THE CIA

The CIA gathers and analyzes five main types of intelligence:

- **Current Intelligence** – Covers day-to-day events
- **Estimative Intelligence** – Predicts events that might happen in the future based on current intelligence
- **Research Intelligence** – Studies a particular issue or subject in detail
- **Scientific and Technical Intelligence** – Covers technologies used by foreign powers and groups
- **Warning Intelligence** – Alerts U.S. policymakers to critical events that would require their immediate attention

CIA agents often use devices such as this miniature video camera to gain information by spying on people.

## CIA Headquarters

CIA Headquarters is located in Langley, Virginia, seven miles from downtown Washington, D.C. In 1955, President Dwight D. Eisenhower authorized $46 million to build the headquarters. Security at CIA headquarters is taken very seriously. Once, a CIA worker forgot his briefcase in a hall of the headquarters. Because the security force did not know to whom the briefcase belonged, they treated it like it was a possible bomb. Security personnel took the briefcase to a concrete lined bomb-disposal room and blew it up—destroying the man's lunch and paperwork!

The CIA has its own private museum. It is located inside CIA Headquarters. The museum has examples of spy equipment, documents, and photographs that at one time were top secret. Since the museum is inside the CIA, it is not open to the public.

Construction of the CIA Headquarters in Langley, Virginia, began in 1959. It was completed in 1961.

Chapter Two

# Inside the CIA

The CIA is a very large, complex organization. It is made up of four divisions: the Directorate of Operations, the Directorate of Science and Technology, the Directorate of Intelligence, and Mission Support Offices. The four divisions report to the director of the CIA.

## The Directorate of Operations

The Directorate of Operations (DO) is the most secretive division of the CIA. Operation officers are the spies who gather information for the DO. The use of spies to obtain information is called espionage. Most people working in the DO live in a foreign country. They are often given fake identities and work at other jobs while gathering information about that area of the world.

Some U.S. government agencies offer public tours of their offices. For security reasons, the CIA is not one of them. Other than CIA employees, few people get to see the inside of CIA Headquarters.

The DO is also referred to as Clandestine Services. Clandestine describes something that is being done covertly, or in secret. Covert CIA actions might involve giving money and weapons to groups that have the same enemies as the United States. Sometimes covert actions are taken to hide the involvement of the United States in an operation, while still protecting America's national security interests.

## The Directorate of Science and Technology

In the movies, James Bond has Q—the man who supplies him with the cool gadgets and equipment he needs to successfully complete his missions. In real life, the CIA has the Directorate of Science and Technology (DS&T) to make its high-tech equipment. Some of this equipment includes recording devices, tiny cameras, and disguises.

The DS&T also collects information. Most of this information is gathered from foreign newspapers, magazines, and TV broadcasts. When it's super-secret information that the CIA requires, the DS&T uses satellites and other electronic technology.

## Eyes in the Sky

Satellites transmit their pictures and recordings electronically to CIA workers many miles away. Some satellites can see through clouds and buildings. Others can sense the presence of people from the heat that their bodies give off. These types of satellites are used to track the movement of enemy armies and find out where enemy weapons are being kept.

### CLASSIFIED INFORMATION

The Directorate of Science and Technology has come up with many unusual places to hide its spy equipment. Sound-recording devices and cameras have been hidden in the oil filters of cars, videotape cassettes, toy trains, batteries, statues, and even teddy bears!

## The Directorate of Intelligence

The Directorate of Intelligence (DI) takes the information collected by the DO and DS&T and carefully studies it. The DI then writes up its conclusions in a variety reports that can be used by the CIA, the president, and congressional leaders. Before the beginning of the Persian Gulf War in 1991, about 180 agents studied information gathered by the DO and DS&T. These agents wrote about five hundred reports for President Bill Clinton to review.

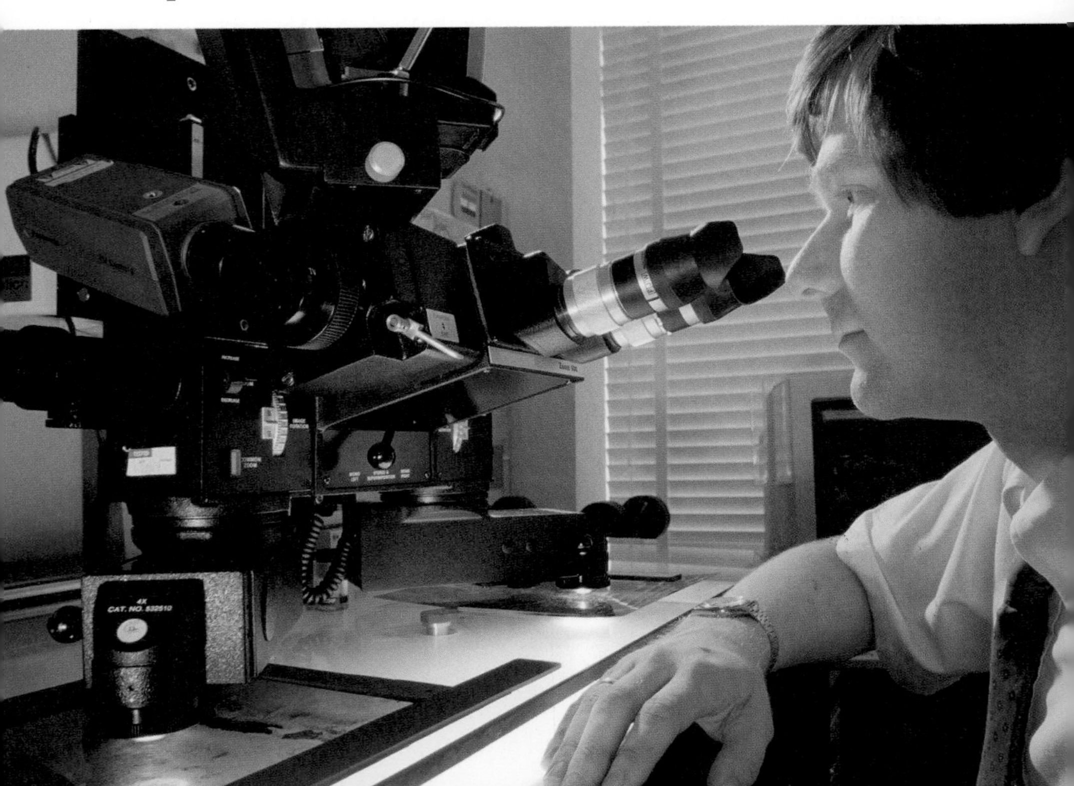

## Mission Support Offices

Mission Support Offices is in charge of giving a helping hand to the other three divisions of the CIA. It keeps all the other divisions running smoothly. Mission Support handles many details, such as hiring and paying employees. It maintains CIA offices by making sure that the they have heat, electricity, phone service, and office equipment.

Several smaller divisions of Mission Support take care of other critical jobs. The Office of Security is responsible for the physical security of CIA headquarters and workers. It protects the director of the CIA and is responsible for detecting listening devices in CIA buildings all over the world. The Office of Medical Services gives physical and psychiatric check-ups to CIA workers. It even works to secretly determine if any world leaders have health problems that may affect their leadership abilities. The Office of Training and Education runs Camp Peary in Williamsburg, Virginia. It trains CIA employees to be spies.

This CIA agent is using a microscope to analyze photographs of the Middle East.

Several other divisions of Mission Support also work to keep the agency running at top speed.

## The Director of Central Intelligence

The head of the CIA is known as the Director of Central Intelligence (DCI). The Director of Central Intelligence reports to the president of the United States and the congressional committees assigned to watch over the CIA. The DCI is in charge of overseeing the entire U.S. intelligence community.

### CLASSIFIED INFORMATION

The President's Daily Brief and many other CIA publications are printed by the CIA—not by another printer. Because so much of what the CIA does is top secret, it has its own printing plant at CIA Headquarters!

The president and the Director of Central Intelligence often work closely together. Here, President George W. Bush (right) meets with CIA Director George J. Tenet in 2001, to discuss issues critical to the security of the United States.

## President's Daily Brief

At the beginning of many of his workdays, the Director of Central Intelligence meets with the president at the White House. The DCI gives the president a report called the President's Daily Brief (PDB) that includes intelligence gathered by the CIA. About half of the important facts included in the PDB are not yet known to the public.

Agency
Network
Management
Center
TOP SECRET

## Chapter Three Getting In

It is believed that about twenty thousand people work for the CIA. There are five main types of positions at the CIA: Professional, Technical, Language, Analytical, and Clandestine Service.

Professional positions include jobs such as lawyers, doctors, mapmakers, and financial planners. Technical positions are jobs for scientists and engineers. These people work with computers, satellites, and electronics. Language positions include translators and language teachers. Analytical jobs are for counter-terrorism, military, and political analysts. Clandestine Service positions deal with the gathering of information. Operations officers work in Clandestine Service.

This CIA agent works in a technical position in the agency's Network Management Center.

## The Application Process

Competition to get a job at the CIA is very strong. Every year, the CIA receives about 200,000 resumés to fill the two thousand jobs that are available. Only about twelve thousand people complete the full process of applying for a position at the CIA.

The job application form for the CIA is over thirty pages long. Applicants are asked to give a lot of information about themselves and their family

CIA employees must be given security clearance each day they go to work. Here, employees insert their identification cards in the entrance gates in the lobby of CIA Headquarters.

members. For example, applicants must list all of the places where they have lived in the last fifteen years. They also have to give a history of all the jobs they have had since they were seventeen years old. Applicants must also take a lie-detector test to prove that all the information they give on their application is true. Examinations are also given to test the job seeker's mental and physical fitness.

The application process is a long one. Depending on the person and the position for which they are applying, the process can take anywhere from two months to more than a year. Everyone who works for the CIA is required to move to the Washington, D.C. area, near CIA Headquarters.

## CLASSIFIED INFORMATION

Many of the people who work at the CIA are not even allowed to reveal where they work. Some family members of CIA employees have no idea that their relative may be a spy!

## Becoming an Operations Officer

Only the best of the best become operations officers. Applicants for this position need the following: a bachelor's degree, an excellent academic record, strong interpersonal skills, the ability to write clearly and accurately, and an interest in world affairs. Many applicants also have a graduate degree, are able to speak a foreign language, have traveled and lived abroad, or have served in the military.

Applicants must go through a rigid interview process and a full background check. If an applicant is accepted by the CIA, he or she trains for two years before going on his or her first overseas assignment. In the first year of training, an officer learns many skills, such as surveillance, electronics, and even how to parachute. In the second year, an officer works at CIA Headquarters in the United States.

In general, the minimum age for employment at the CIA is eighteen years old. The maximum age for applicants to the Clandestine Service is thirty-five. Applicants must be U.S. citizens.

## CLASSIFIED INFORMATION

Most CIA operations officers have diplomatic immunity when they are working in a foreign country. Diplomatic immunity means that a person from one country cannot be tried for breaking the laws of another country. In the event that a CIA operations officer is caught spying by another country, he or she will usually be sent back to the United States.

Chapter Four

# The CIA in Action

The CIA has helped prevent wars and save countless lives around the world. Its spy efforts have also supplied the United States with information vital to the nation's security. Yet many people believe that the CIA has been guilty of abusing its power. Let's take a look at some of the CIA's most famous cases—and examine some of the criticism directed at the agency.

## The Cold War

In the years following World War II, much of the CIA's work was directed toward spying on the Soviet Union. The United States and the Soviet Union were involved in a war of ideas called the Cold War. The Cold War was a heated rivalry between the United States and its allies, and the Soviet Union and other communist countries.

This small camera was taken from an agent of the Soviet Union's spy agency, the KGB, in 1948.

## Tunnel of Secrets: The Berlin Tunnel

After World War II, the city of Berlin, Germany, was divided into two halves. Communists controlled East Berlin while West Berlin was democratic. In 1953, the CIA built a tunnel which allowed agents to gain access to 432 Soviet telephone lines in East Berlin. The telephone lines connected the Soviet high command in East Berlin to Soviet intelligence headquarters in the city, and to Moscow, in the Soviet Union. Tapping into the telephone calls gave the CIA important information about the military plans of the Soviet Union. It kept the United States informed and alerted the CIA to possible threats to U.S. security.

### CLASSIFIED INFORMATION

The Berlin Tunnel was dug 15 feet (4.8 meters) underground. It was 600 yards (549 m) long and 6 feet (1.83 m) high.

This photograph, taken in Germany, shows a Soviet military officer pointing to a spot where he claims U.S. agents had tapped into Soviet telephone lines.

## Trouble in Cuba: The Cuban Missile Crisis

In 1961, the Directorate of Science and Technology made a shocking—and disturbing—discovery. Photographs taken by U.S. reconnaissance planes showed that the Soviet Union had supplied Cuba, a communist nation, with nuclear missiles. Cuba, only 90 miles (144.8 kilometers) from the U.S. mainland, would soon be able to set up and launch these missiles at the United States. The CIA provided this information to President John F. Kennedy and his staff. President Kennedy threatened the Soviet Union with military action if the missiles were not removed. He sent warships out to sea to prevent the

Soviets from shipping any more missiles to Cuba. In the tense days that followed, people around the world feared that a nuclear war was about to happen. Fortunately, the Soviets backed down, finally pulling their missiles out of Cuba. The CIA's work had helped remove a nuclear threat to the United States.

## A New Threat

In time, hostilities between the United States and the Soviet Union began to ease. The CIA, however, was forced to turn its attention to another threat—international terrorism.

### The Bug in the Sewer

In 1976, seven terrorists took over the Indonesian consulate in Amsterdam, in the Netherlands. The Netherlands, or Holland, is ruled by the Dutch government. The terrorists were armed with explosives, guns, and knives. They demanded that the Dutch government recognize the non-existent Republic of South Molucca, in Indonesia.

This photograph was taken from an airplane in 1962. It shows nuclear weapons in Cuba that were supplied by the Soviet Union.

This miniature listening device is an important piece of spy equipment.

They took thirty-six hostages—twenty-one of them were children attending school in the building. The terrorists placed explosives in a room and threatened to blow everyone up if their demands were not met. The CIA was called to action.

With the approval of the Dutch government, a CIA agent crawled through a sewer pipe and into the basement of the building where the hostages were being held. There, he planted a bug, or listening device. Several days later, a gunshot was heard in the building. Police got ready to enter the building. If they did, many of the hostages might have lost their lives during a gun battle. Amazingly, the bug had picked up that the gunshot was not the sound of a hostage being shot. It was the sound of a gun going off after accidentally being dropped by one of the terrorists. The police then waited for the terrorists to make a move. After fifteen days the terrorists gave up. No lives were lost thanks to the work of the CIA.

## The Ultimate Price

U.S. intelligence sources pinpointed the terrorist organization Al Qaeda as the one responsible for the September 11, 2001, attacks against the United States. Al Qaeda was based mainly in Afghanistan, and was supported by the ruling Taliban government. When the United States and its allies took military action in Afghanistan, CIA covert operatives were sent to assist. Operatives are believed to have supplied weapons, training, and intelligence to the Afghan people fighting the Taliban. Among those CIA operatives was Johnny Michael Spann. Spann was questioning Taliban prisoners when a riot broke out. He was killed by Taliban prisoners as they tried to escape. Spann, a former U.S. Marine, was the seventy-ninth CIA agent to have died in the line of duty.

## Under Fire

Over the years, the CIA has drawn heavy criticism for the way it has conducted several of its covert spy operations. Many people believe that the agency has become too powerful and too secretive. Because of these concerns, special groups now oversee the work of the CIA to make sure that it does not abuse its power and authority.

### Shot Down Over Russia

In 1960, a U.S. U-2 spy plane was shot down over Russia. The plane was piloted for the CIA by Francis Gary Powers. Powers was once an air force pilot. He was taking photos to see if the Soviet Union had built more nuclear weapons than the United States. The CIA assured President Dwight D. Eisenhower that evidence that the U-2 was a spy plane would never be found. Based on the CIA's advice, President Eisenhower denied that the plane was on a spy mission. The Soviets, however, soon presented

Johnny Michael Spann was thirty-two years old when he was killed during the prison riot in Afghanistan on November 25, 2001.

Powers' spy photos. The U.S. government was caught in a lie. Powers was taken prisoner and sentenced to ten years in a Soviet jail. He was soon exchanged for a Soviet spy that the United States had captured. The incident greatly embarrassed the U.S. government and the CIA.

## Abuse of Power

In 1967, a CIA inspector general's report told of the many secret CIA attempts to assassinate Cuban premier Fidel Castro. News of other abuses of power began to come out. For example, it was discovered that the CIA had made plans to assassinate the leader of the Congo (now the Democratic Republic of Congo), in Africa. Today, plots to assassinate foreign leaders are not allowed. In 1964, the agency tried to influence the outcome of an election in Chile. It did not want Salvador Allende, who was considered unfriendly toward the United States, to win the election. Allende lost, but six years later, he won the next election. The CIA then backed a military uprising to prevent Allende from taking power. The uprising failed and Allende took power.

Other abuses of power were directed toward citizens of the United States. In 1953, the CIA had begun inspecting mail going to and coming from the Soviet Union. Some of this activity broke federal laws. By 1973, the CIA was inspecting 2.3 million

Francis Gary Powers looks at wreckage of his downed U-2 plane in Moscow.

pieces of mail a year. They photographed 33,000 envelopes and opened 8,700 of them.

In 1967, the CIA started a program to spy on U.S. citizens who were thought to be a threat to the security of the United States. About 300,000 American citizens and organizations were named in the files that the CIA put together. This type of espionage was against the rules of the CIA.

Abuses of power such as these led to the establishment of the Church Committee in 1975. This congressional committee, led by Senator Frank Church, looked closely into the work of the CIA. The result was tighter control of the CIA by government officials. Today, the National Security Council, the Senate Select Committee on Intelligence, and the House Permanent Select Committee on Intelligence, as well as other committees, closely oversee the CIA's work.

The stars on this wall at the entrance of the original CIA Headquarters building honor the seventy-nine men and women who have died while working for the CIA. The names of thirty-five of these people still have not been revealed.

## The Future of the CIA

The events of September 11, 2001, have changed the way the CIA operates. The CIA has been ordered by government officials to share its information more openly with other agencies, such as the Federal Bureau of Investigation (FBI).

Gathering information from places around the world has never been more important. Yet the CIA will be there to do the job it has done for over fifty years. The CIA must meet the challenge of protecting Americans and their allies around the world, while still working within the laws of the United States. It is a challenge the CIA is prepared to meet.

# New Words

**clandestine** when something is done in secret

**consulate** the offices used by a government official from one country who has gone to another country to live and work

**directorate** a division or team that is dedicated to handling one type of activity

**espionage** the use of spies to gain secret information about another government

**intelligence** the end product of information that has been collected and analyzed

**operation** a mission that has been carefully planned

**reconnaissance** having to do with the exploration of an area, usually to gather information about military forces

# New Words

**resumés** outlines of one's job history and experience

**sabotage** the intentional destruction of property or disruption of work

**security** actions taken to protect sensitive information and the safety of people against enemy action

**Soviet Union** a former country covering eastern Europe and northern Asia that was ruled by a communist form of government

**strategic** having to do with the use of skillful planning to achieve a goal

**surveillance** the close observation of a person or group

**terrorism** the use of fear or violence to reach a goal

# For Further Reading

Gaines, Ann G. *Terrorism*. Philadelphia, PA: Chelsea House, 1999.

January, Brendan. *The CIA.* Danbury, CT: Franklin Watts, 2002.

Kessler, Ronald. *Inside the CIA*. New York: Pocket Books, 1994.

Mello, Tara Baukus. *The Central Intelligence Agency.* Philadelphia, PA: Chelsea House, 2000.

Melton, H. Keith. *The Ultimate Spy Book.* New York: DK Publishing, 1996.

Ziff, John. *Espionage and Treason.* Philadelphia, PA: Chelsea House, 2000.